PRETTY LITTLE THING
COLORING BOOK
MIDNIGHT EDITION

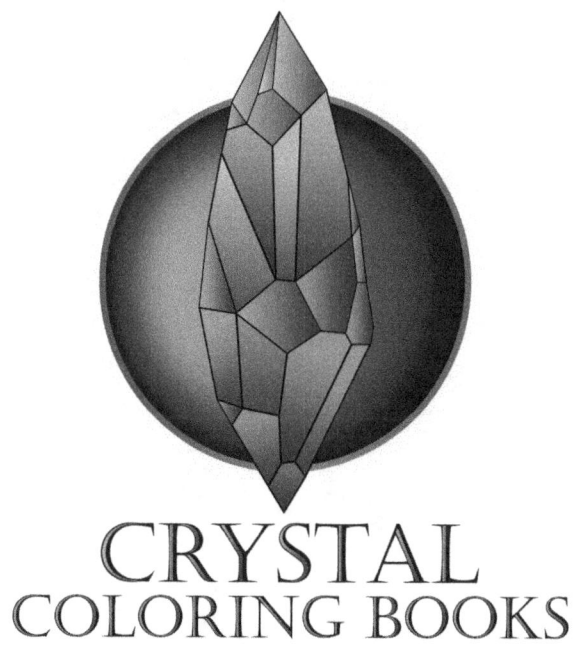

CRYSTAL
COLORING BOOKS

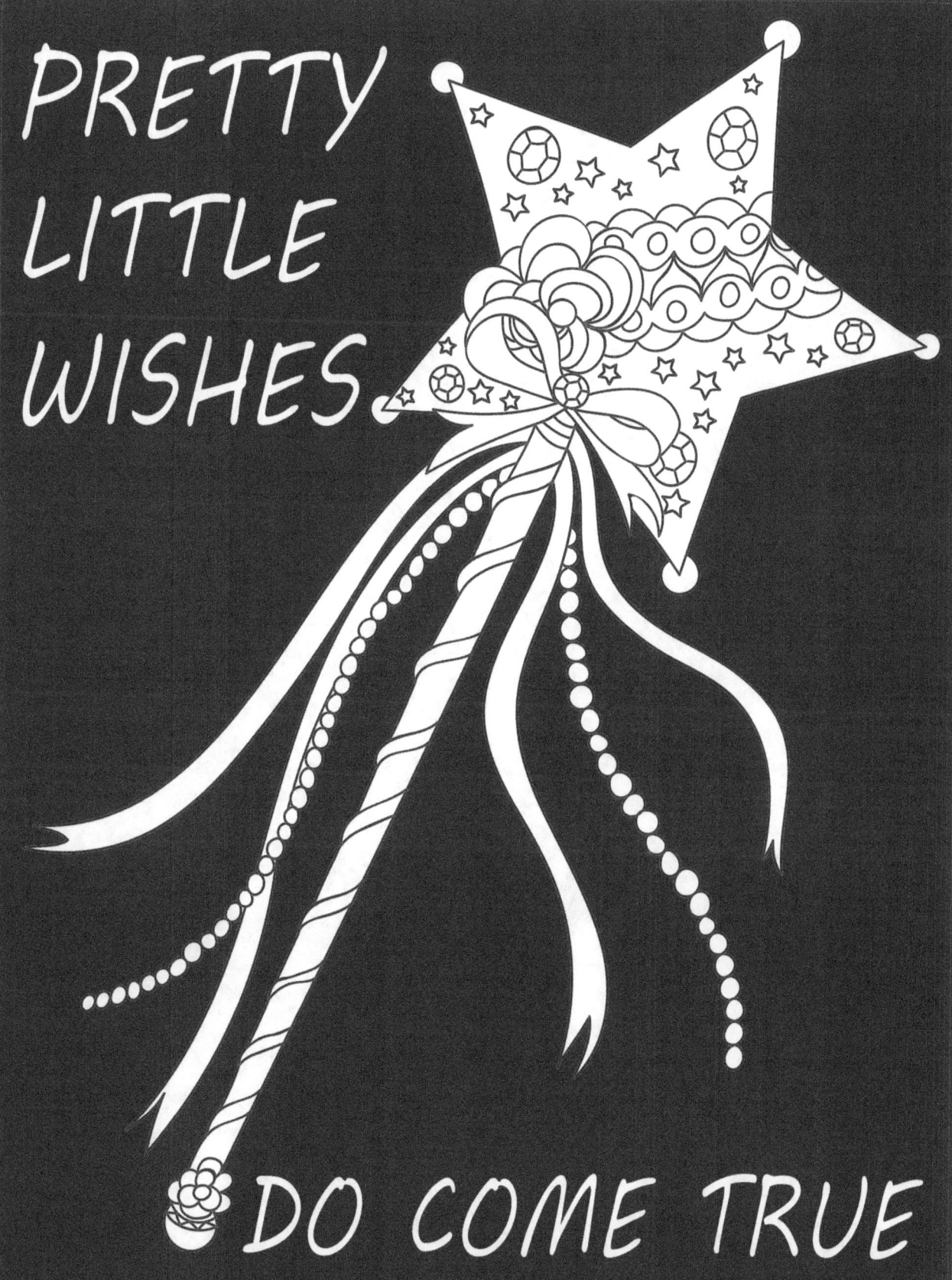

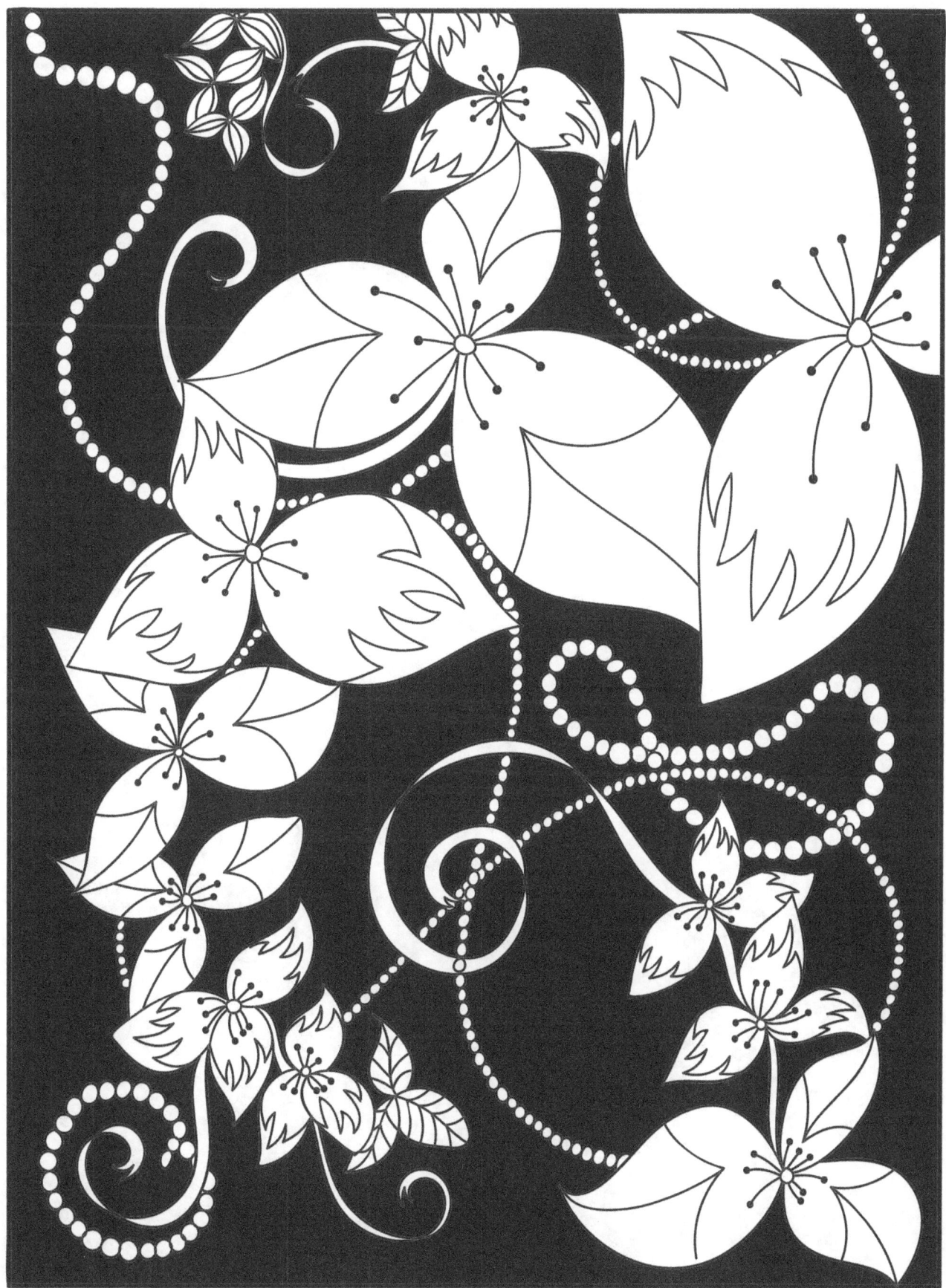

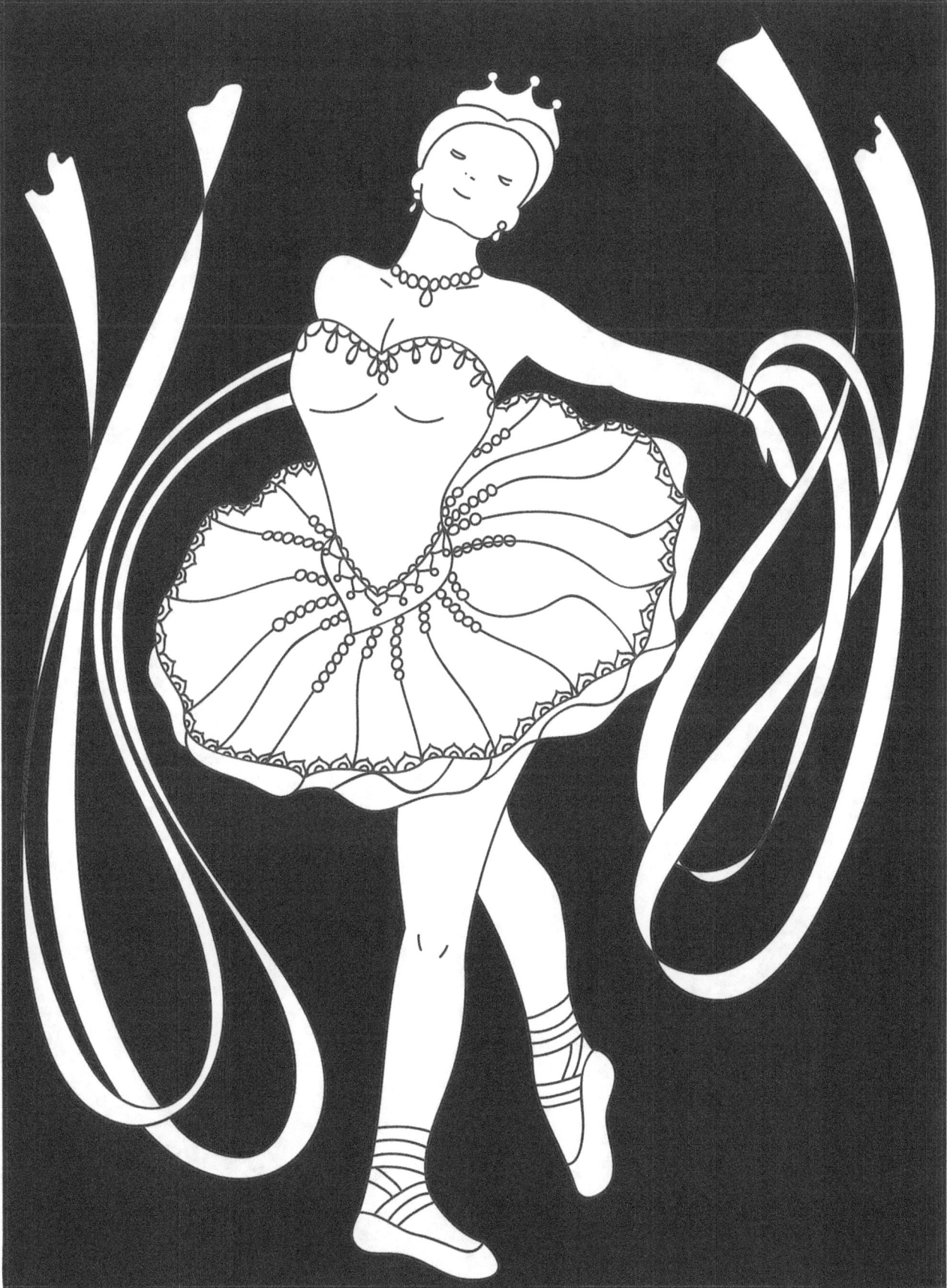

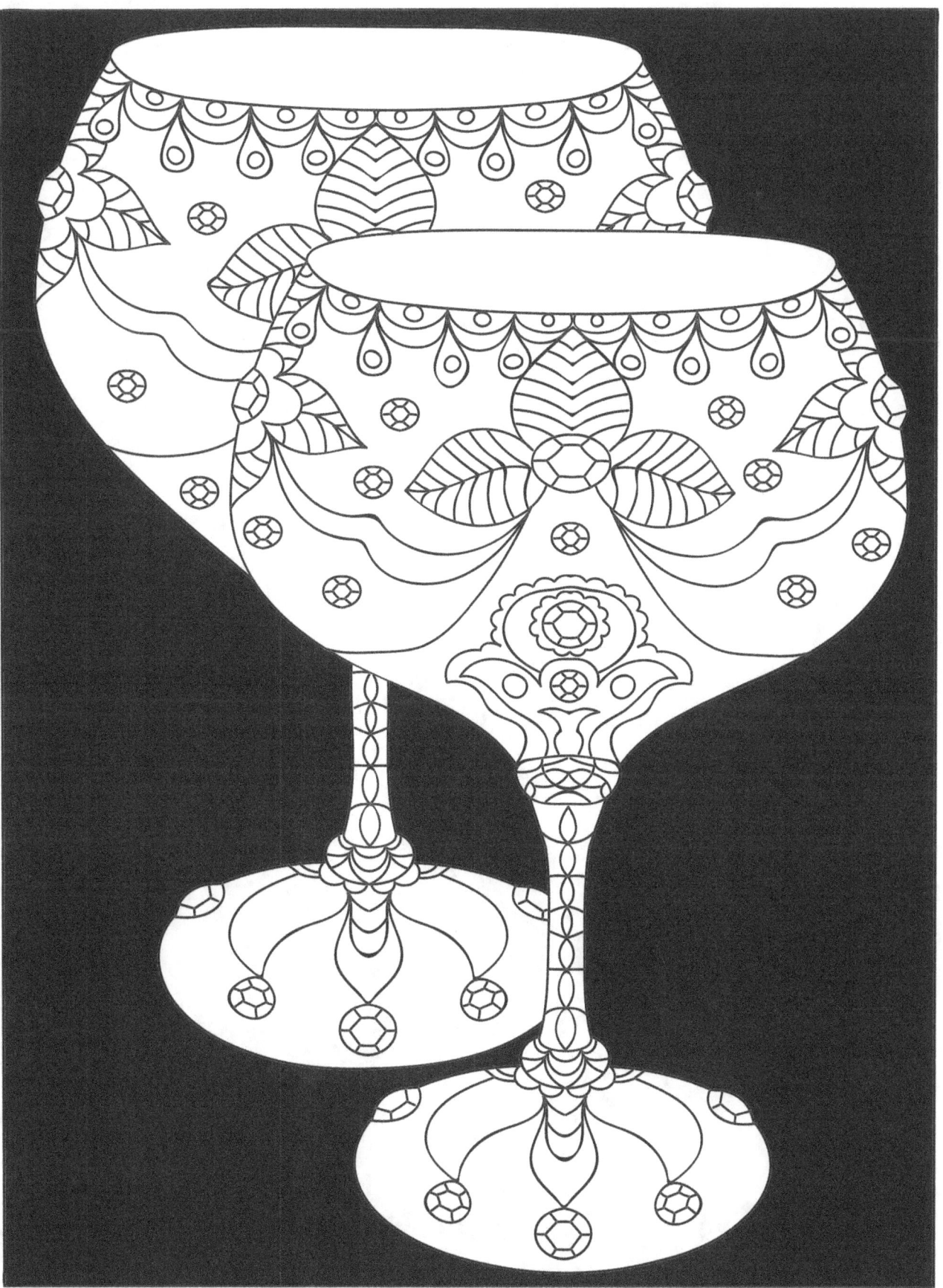

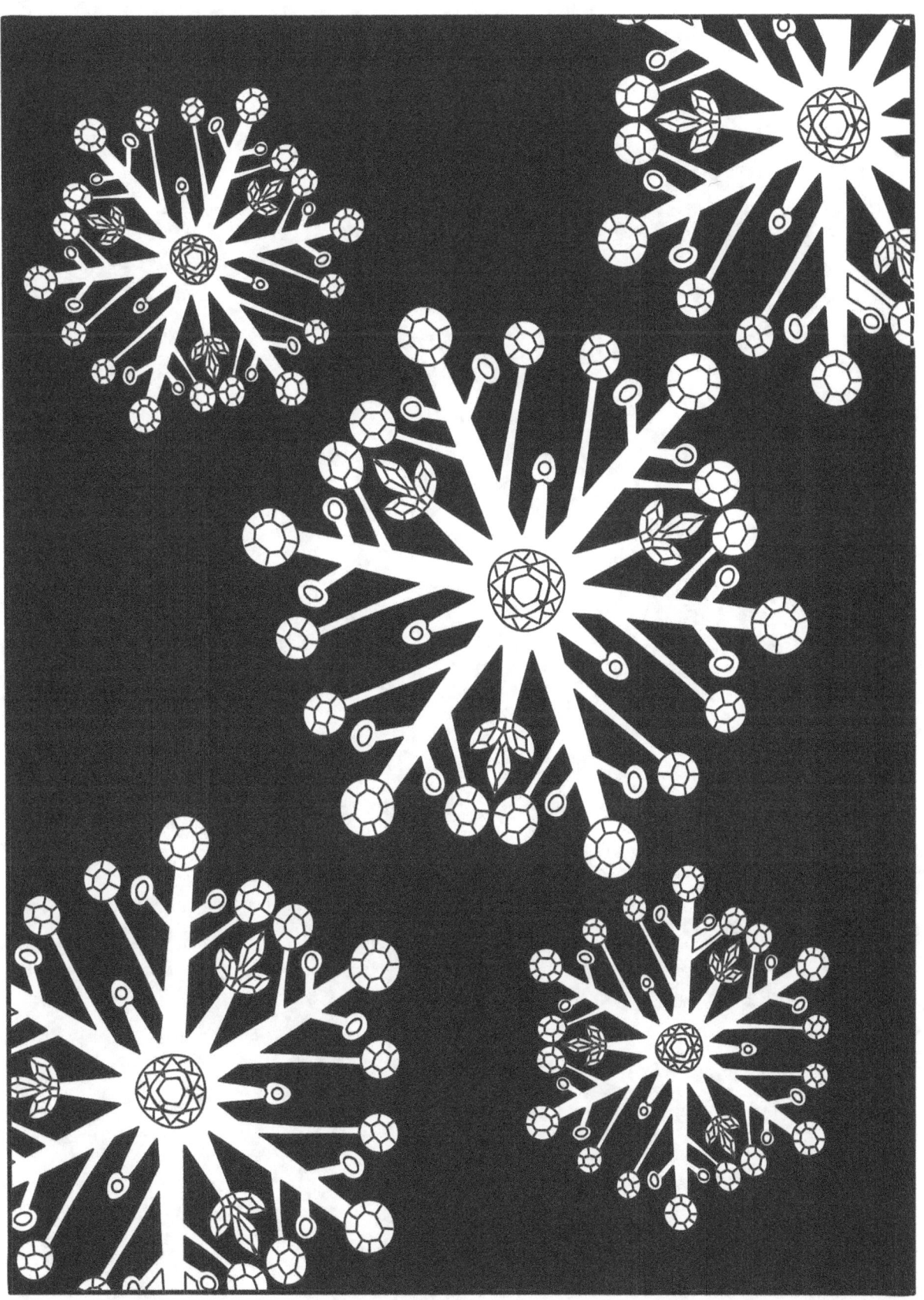

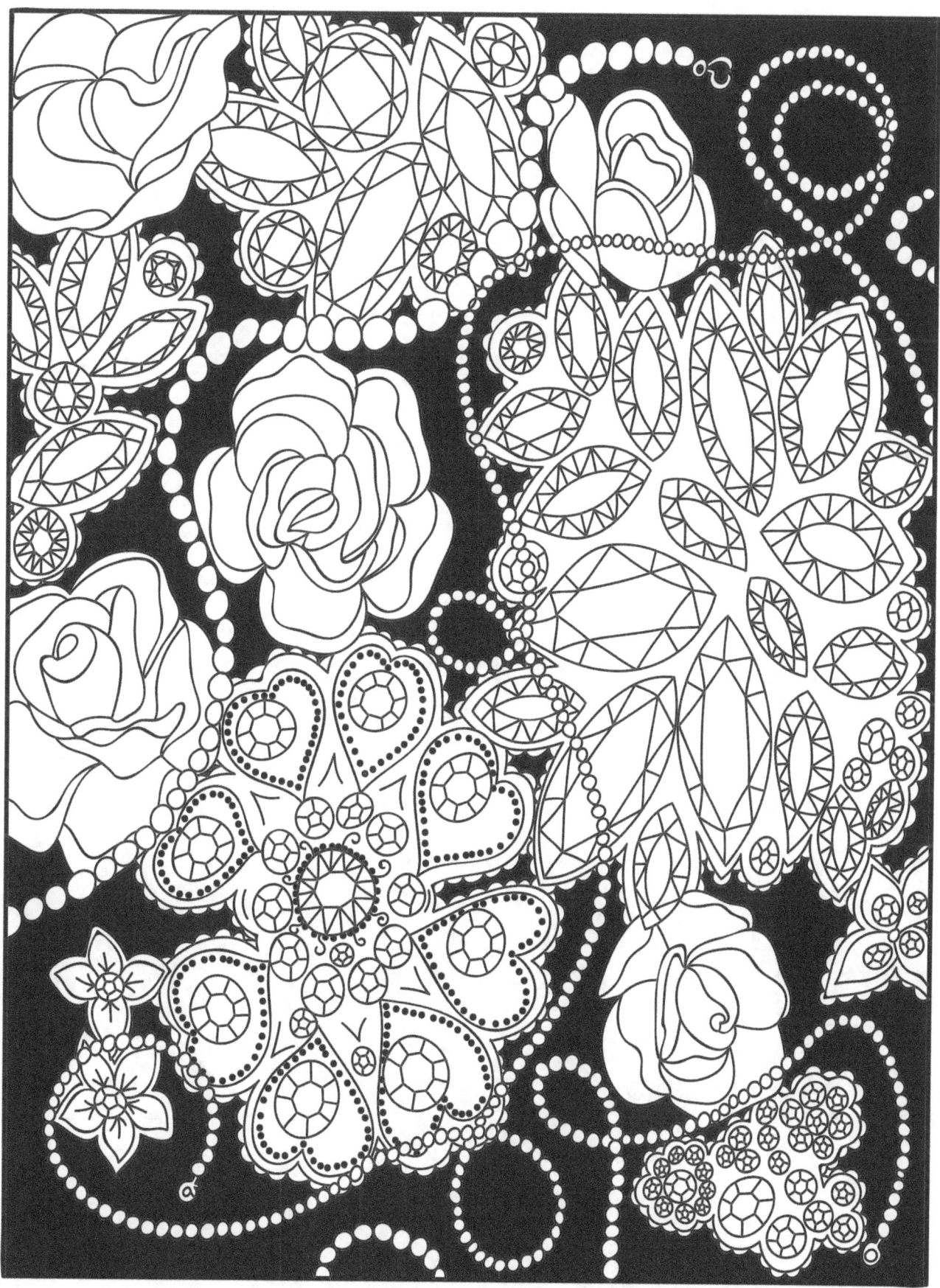

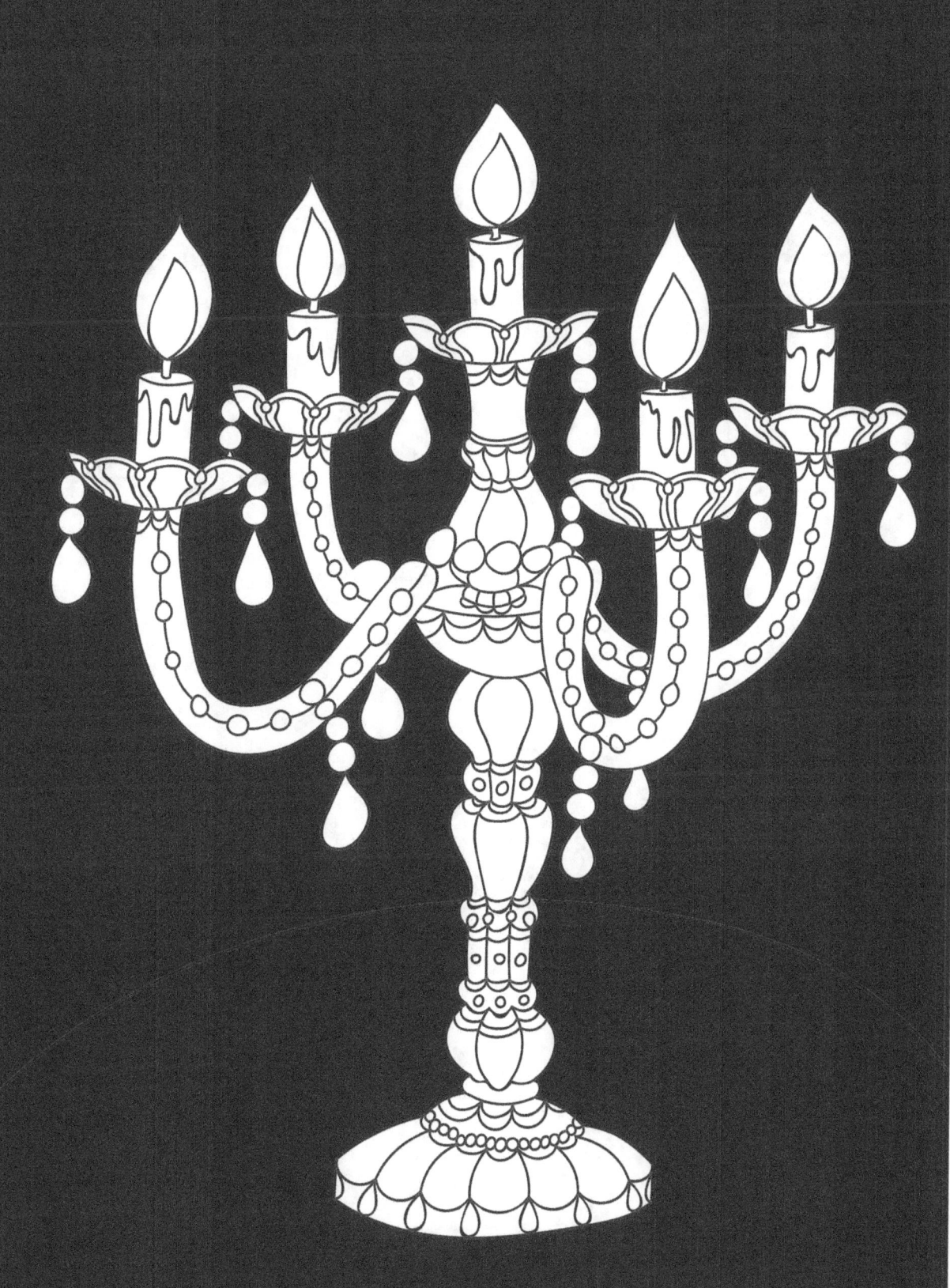

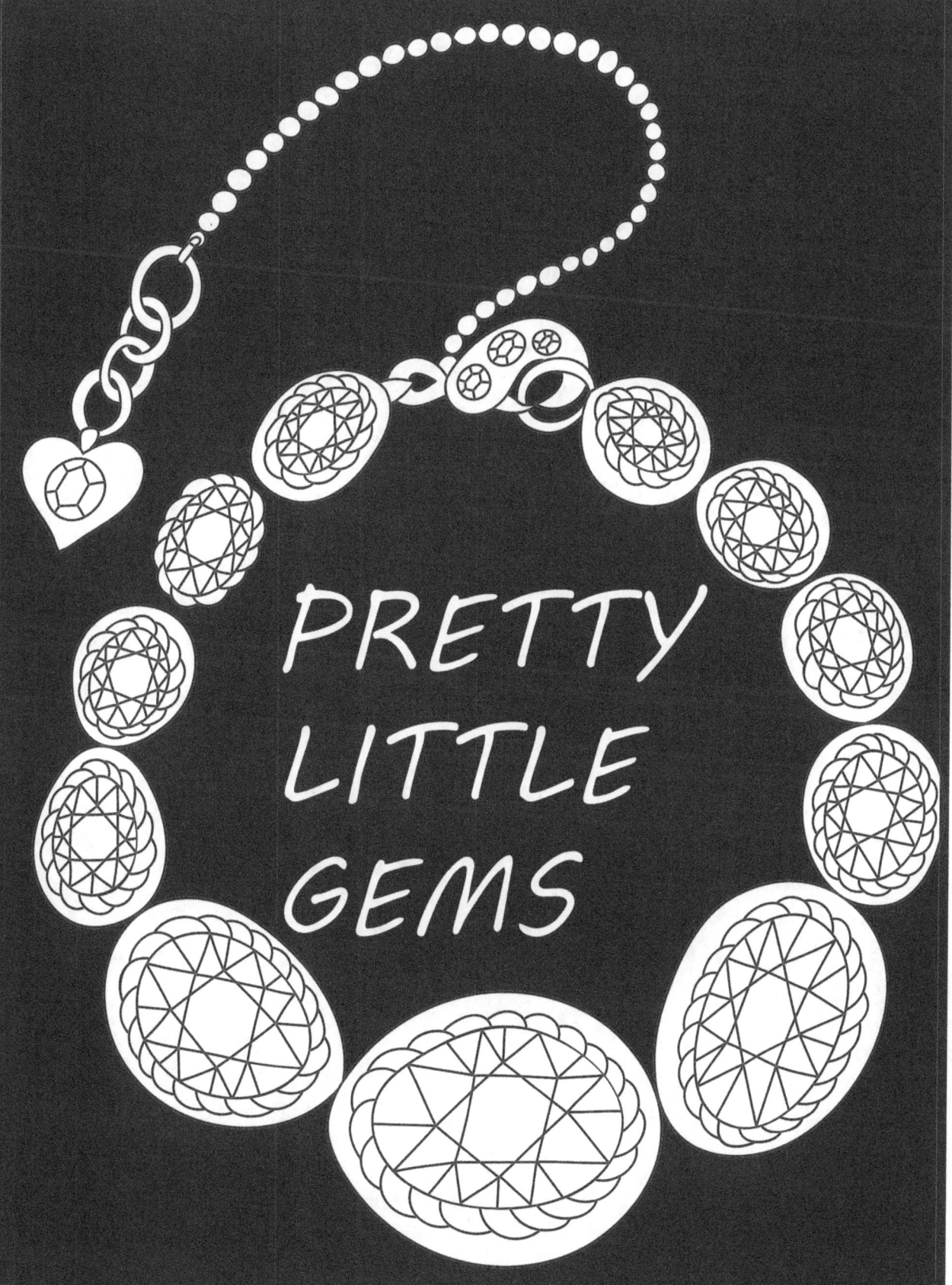

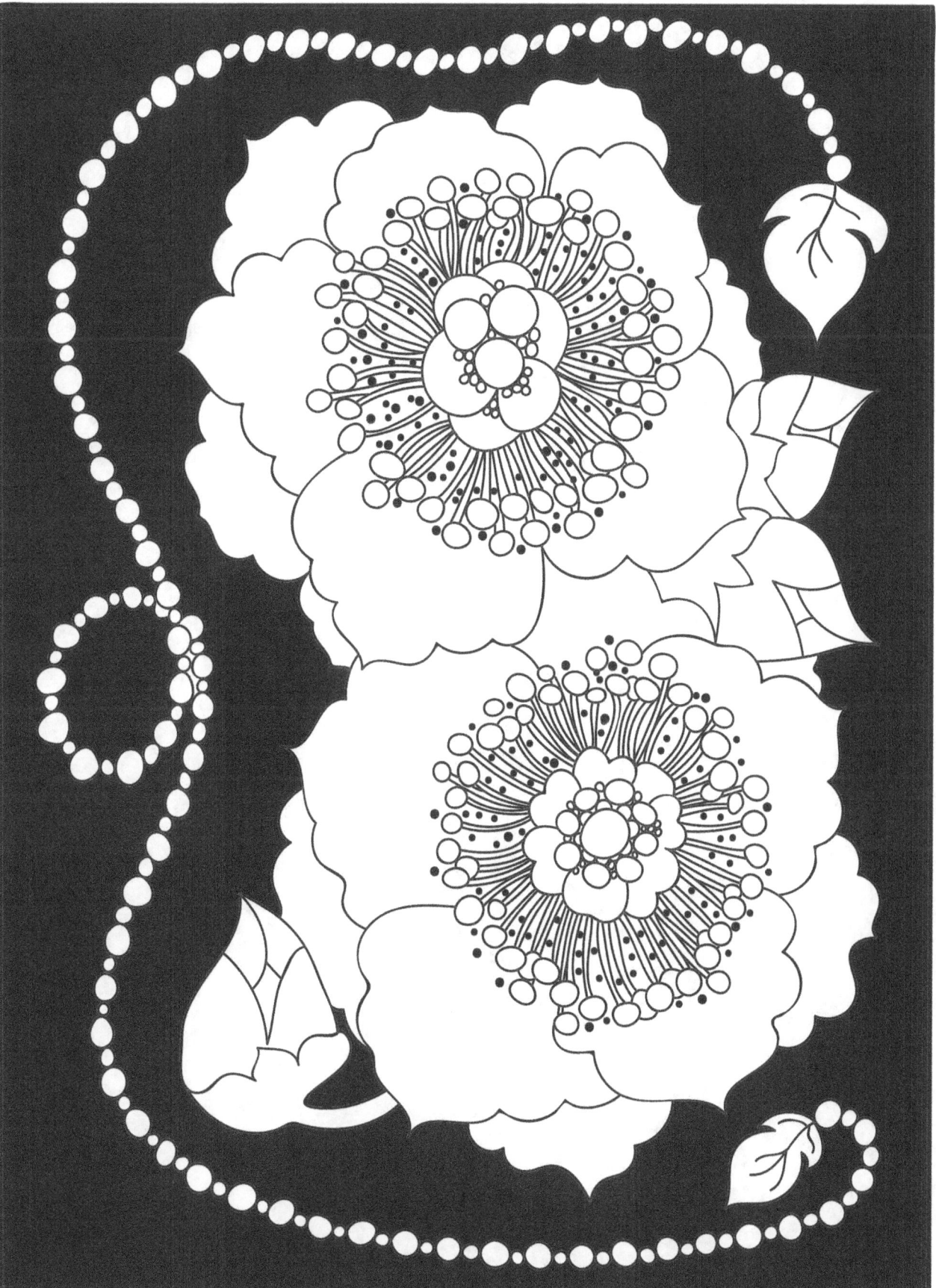

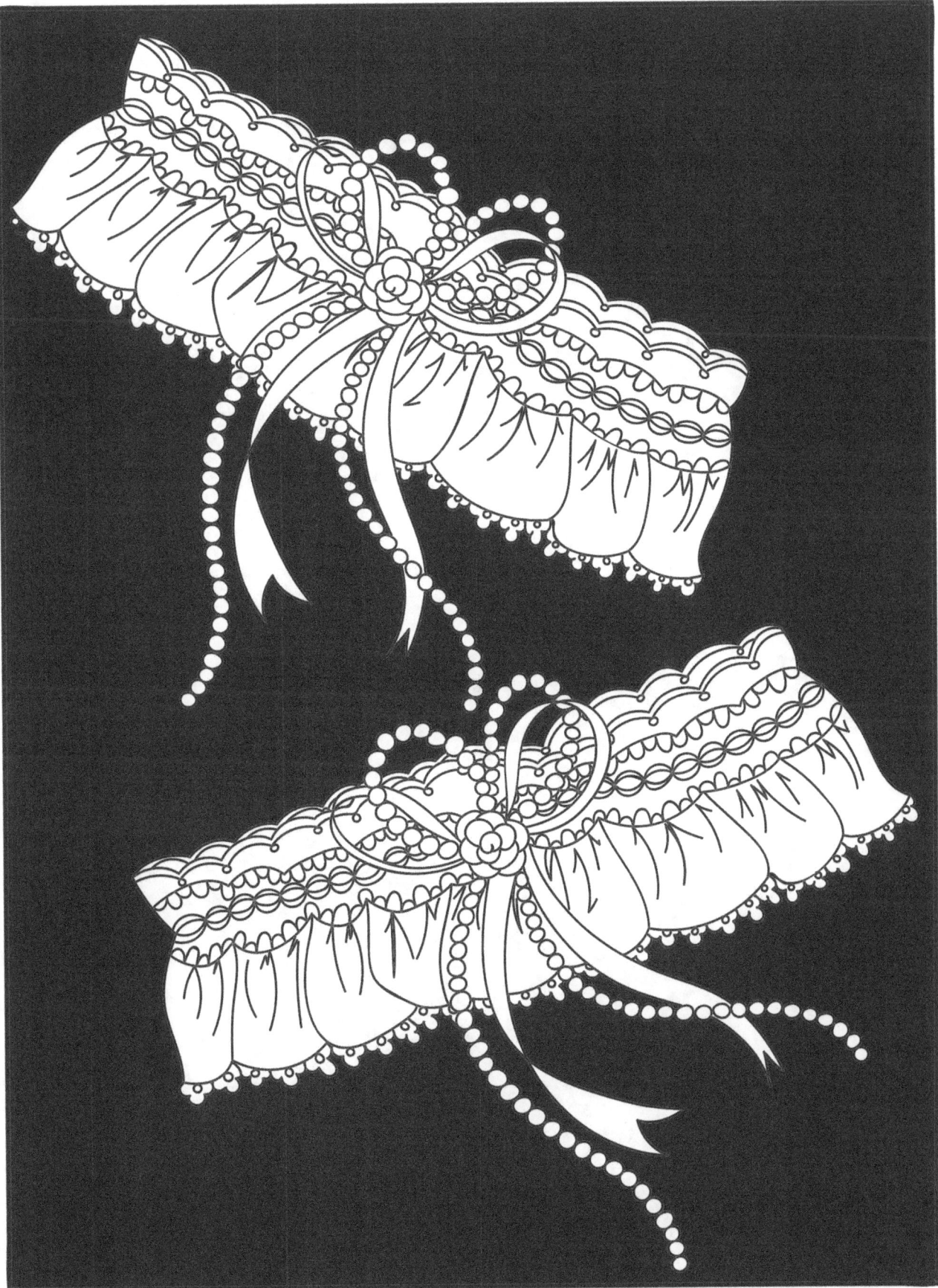

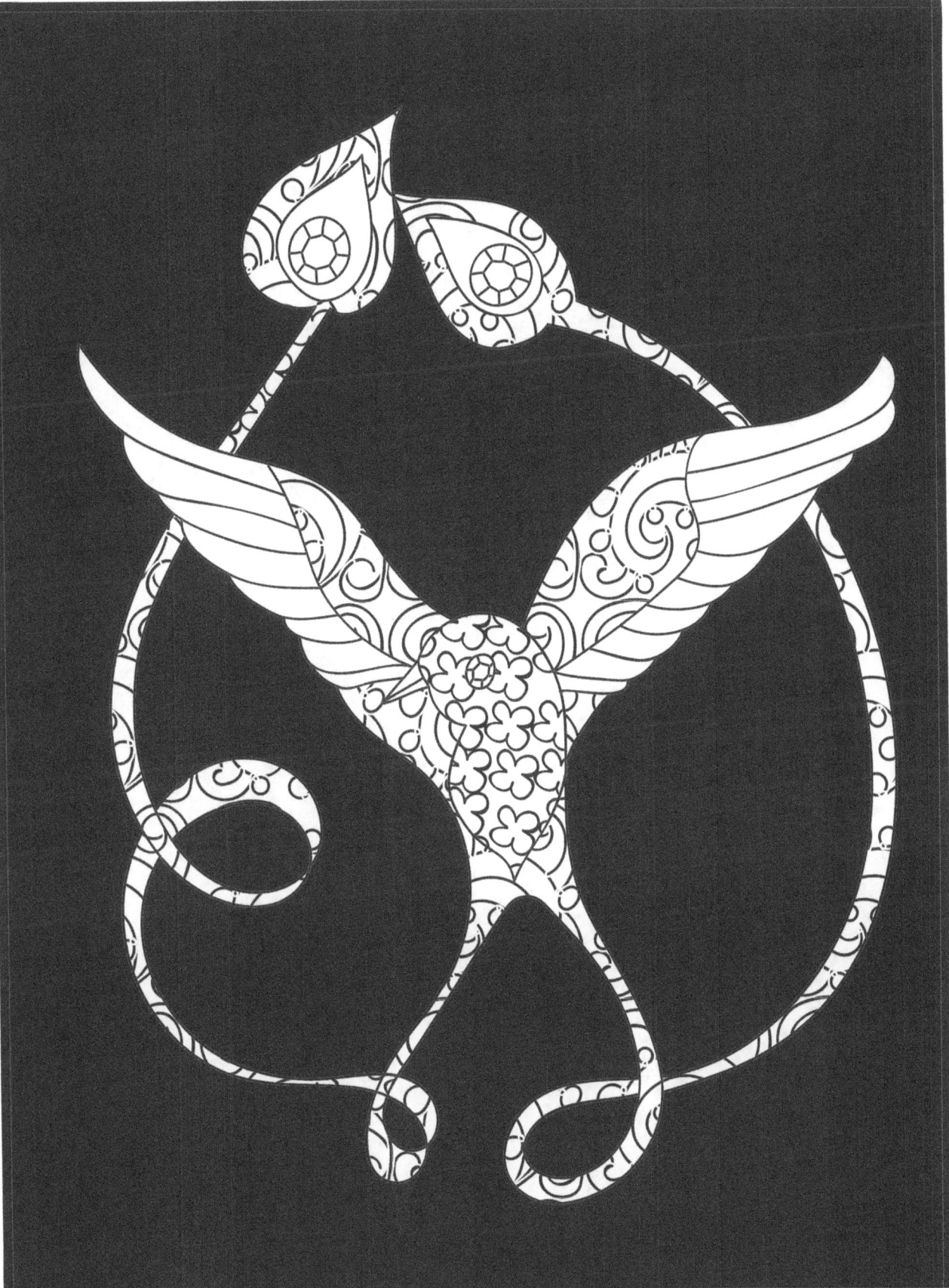

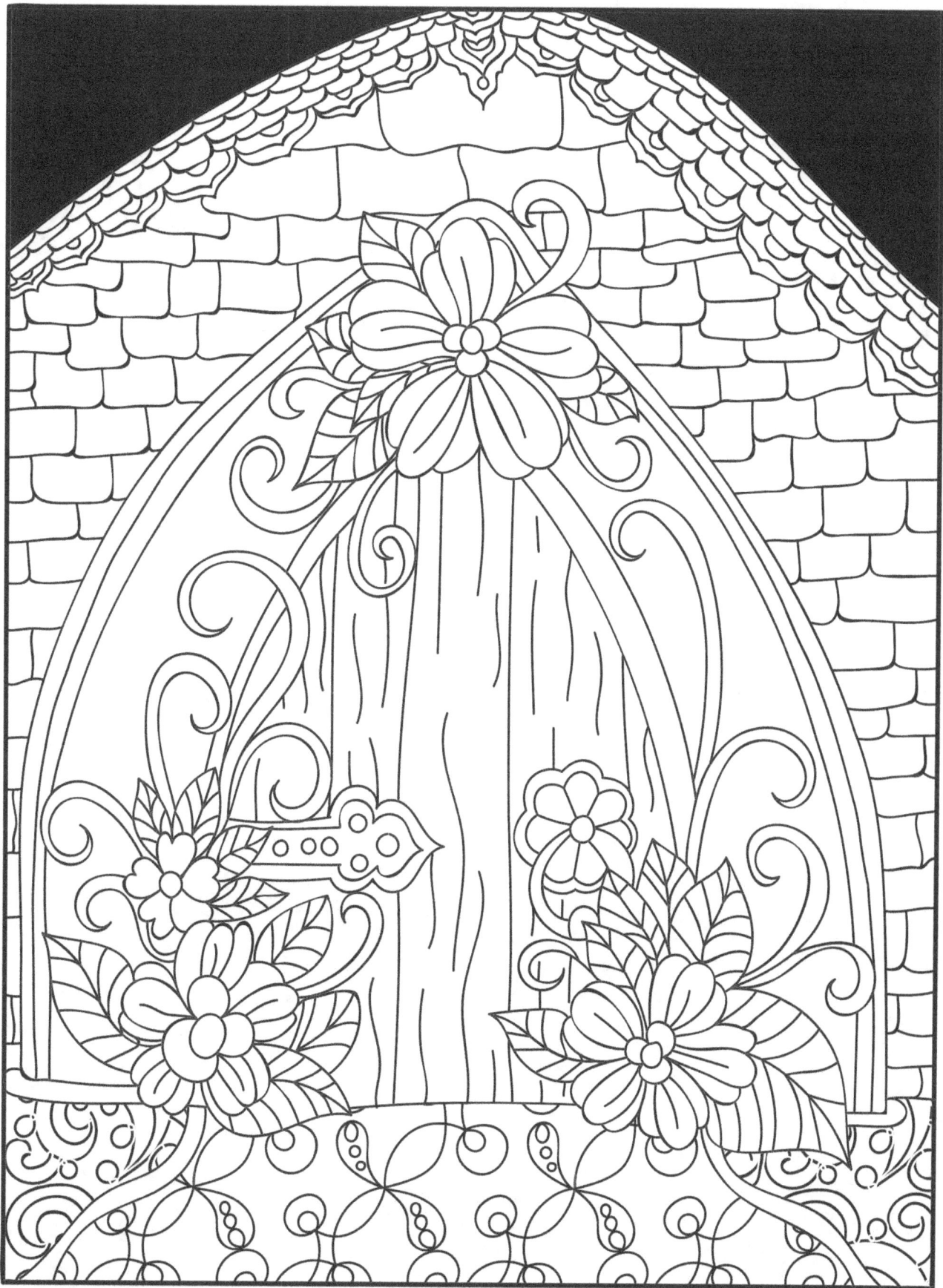

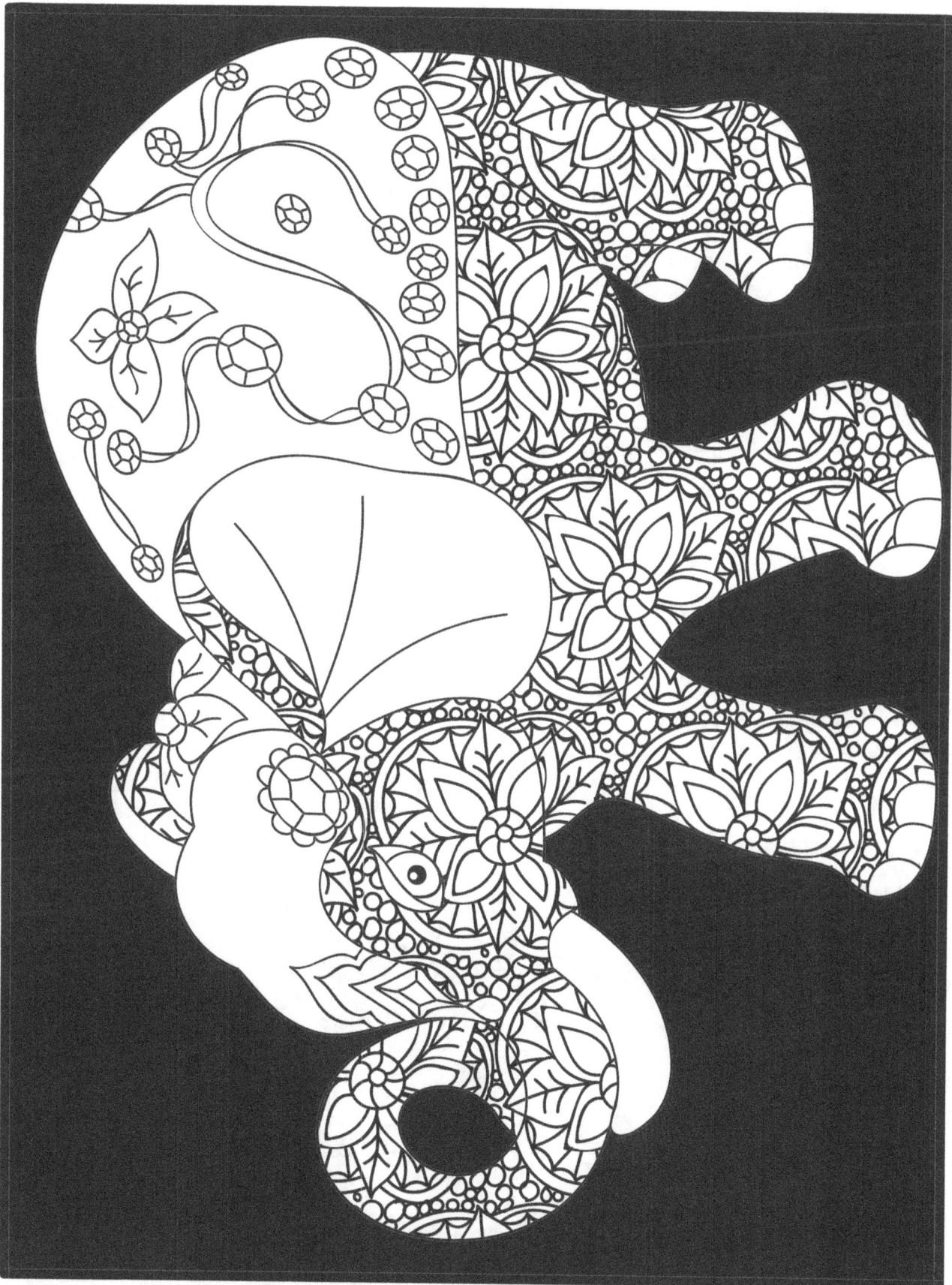

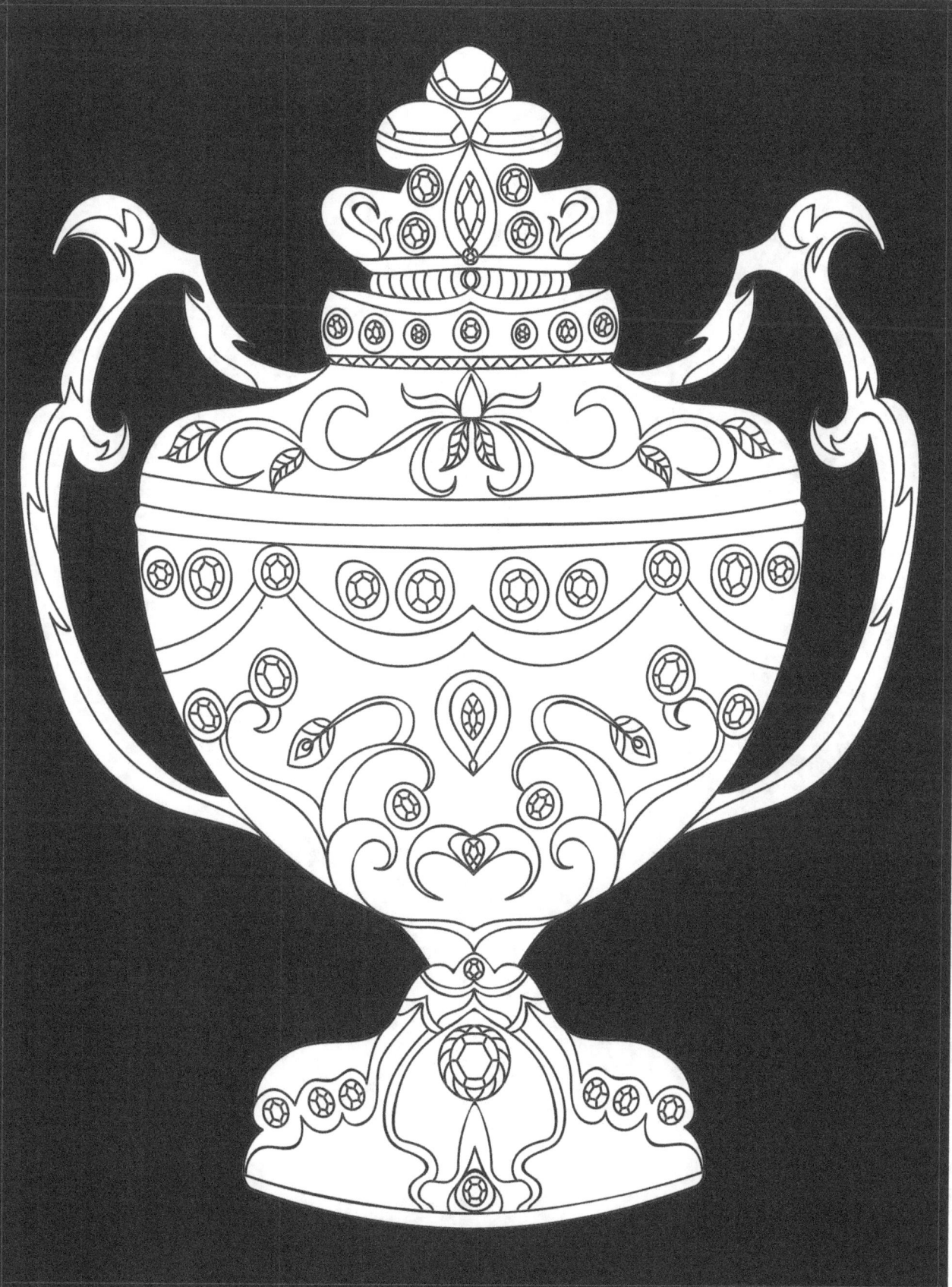

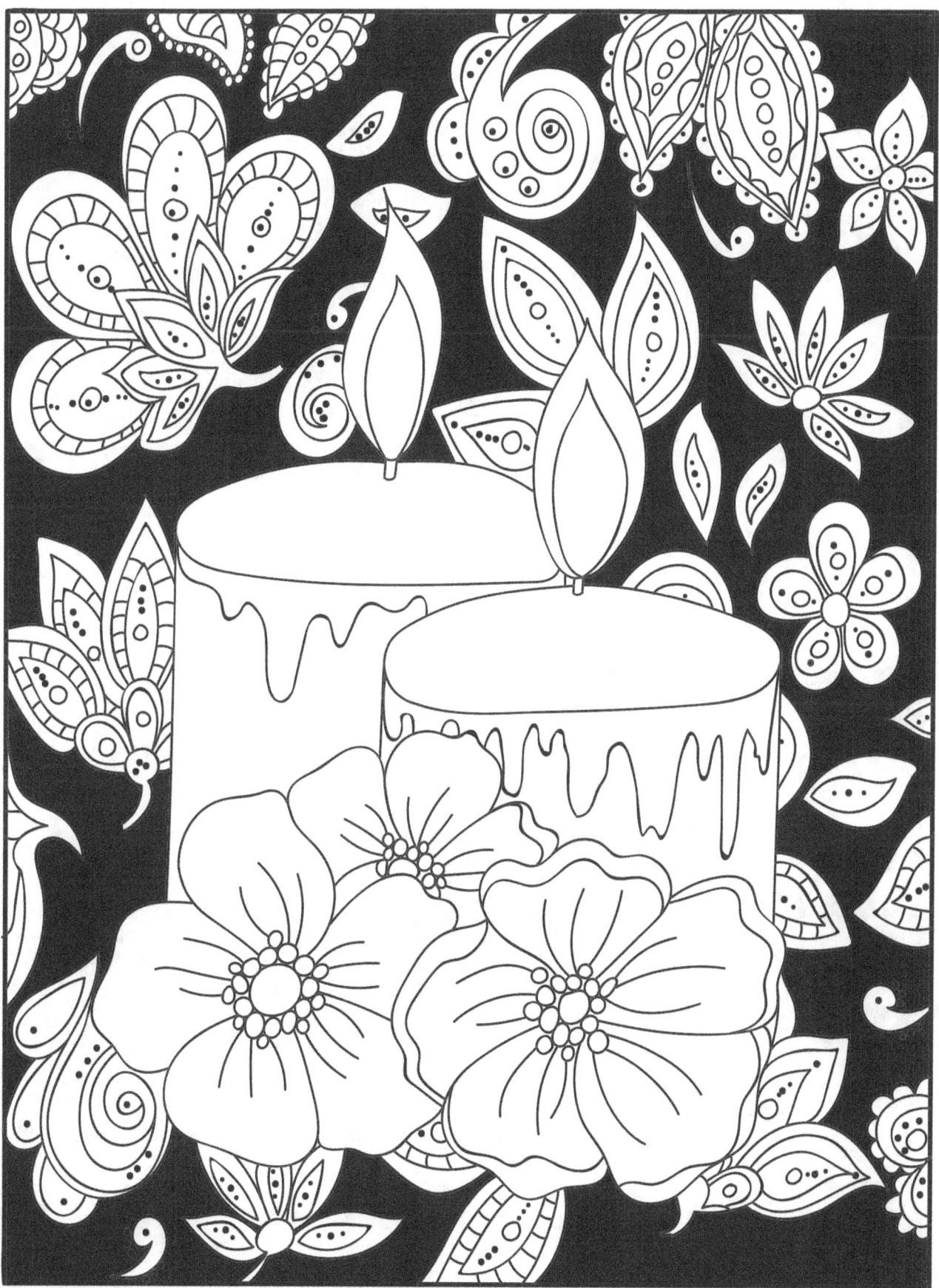

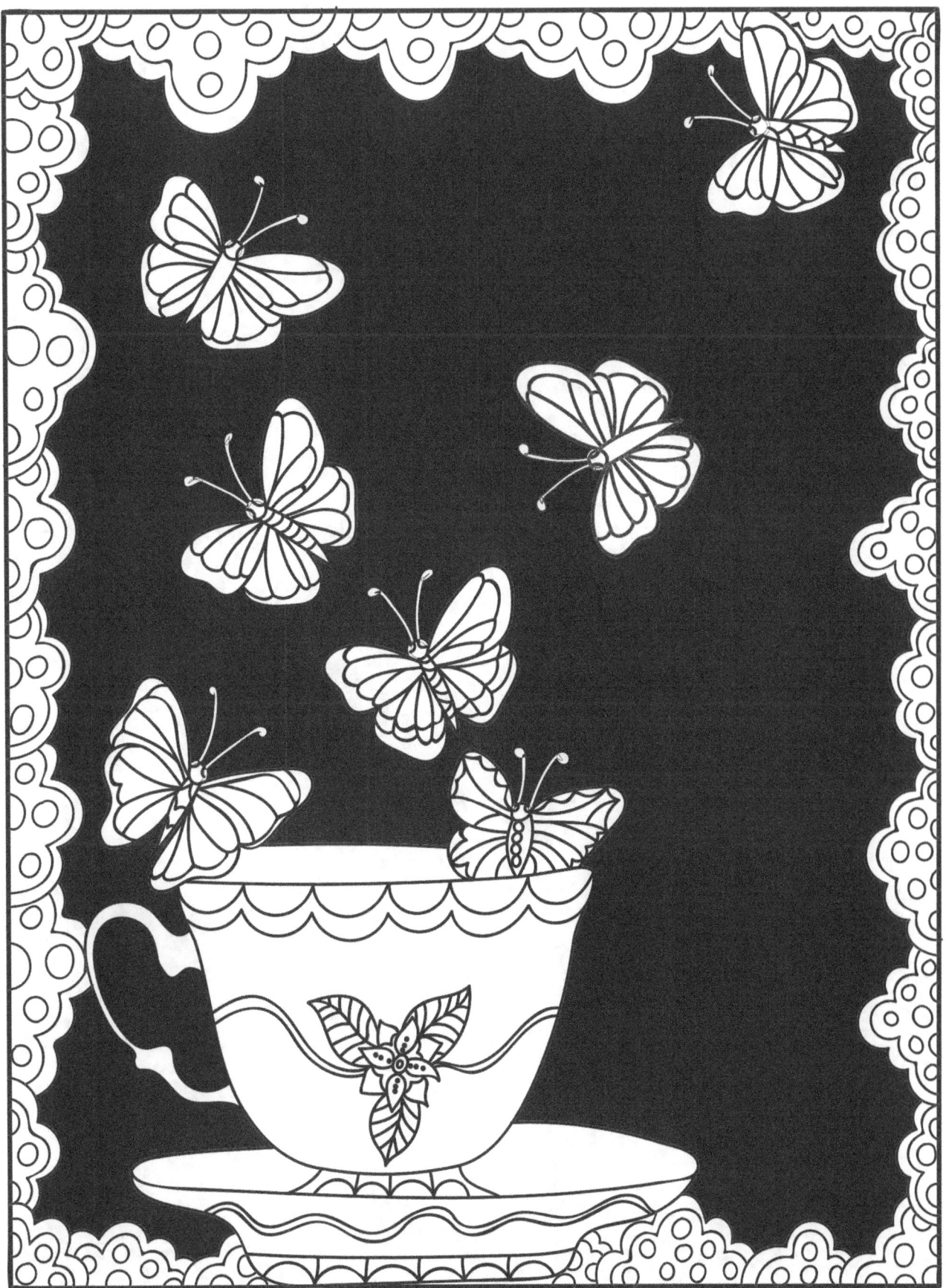

YOU ARE A PRETTY

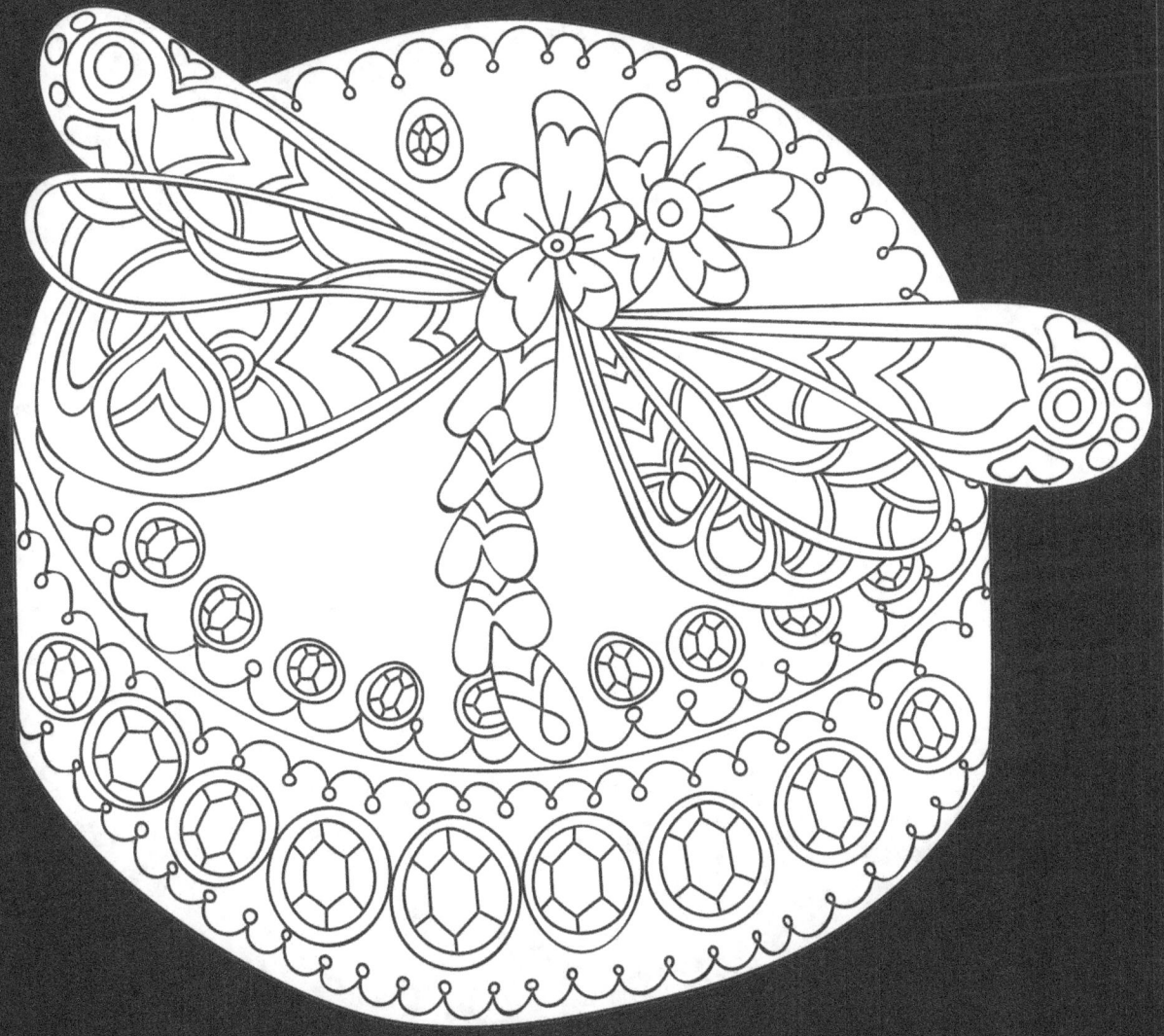

LITTLE THING

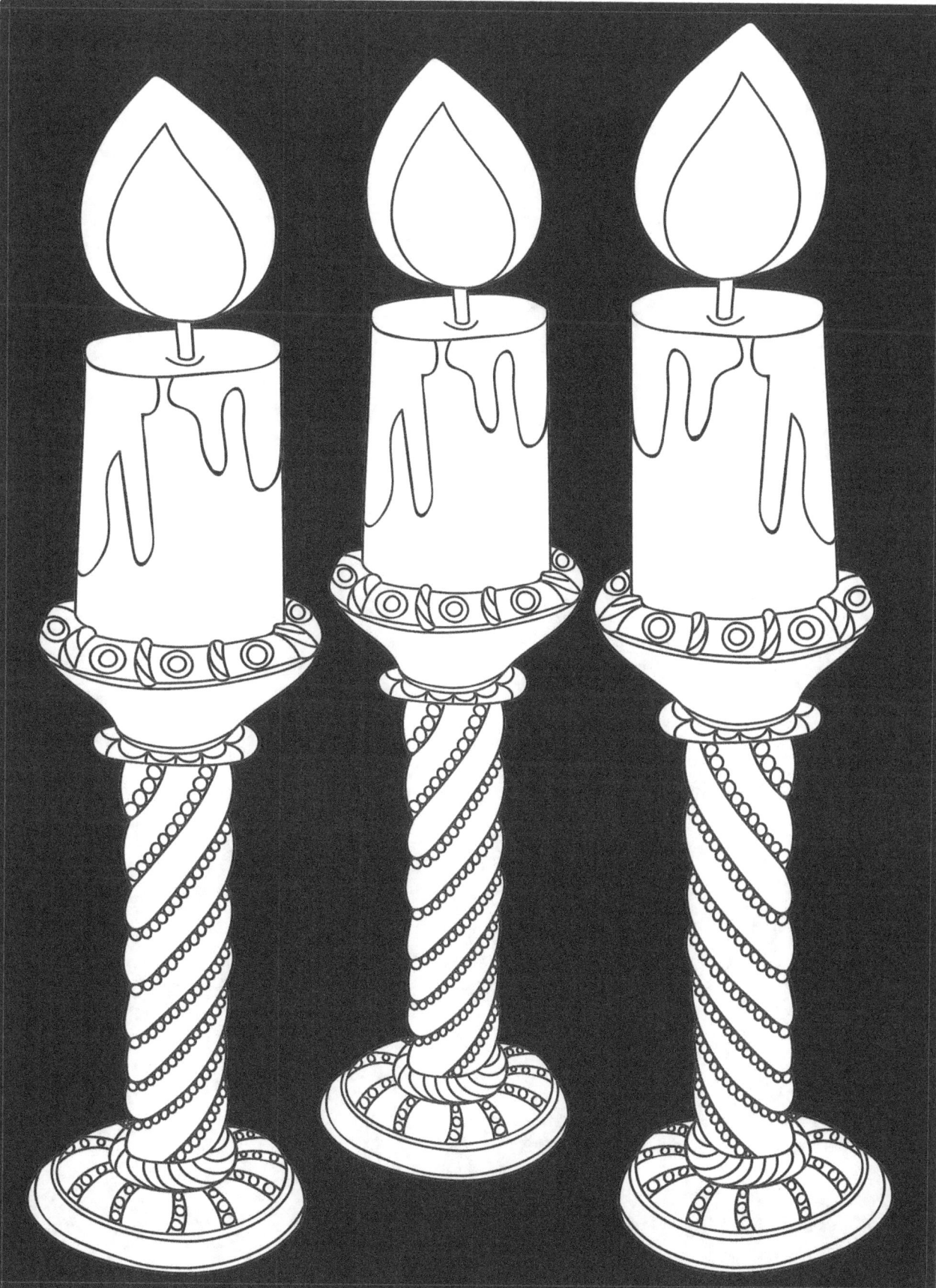

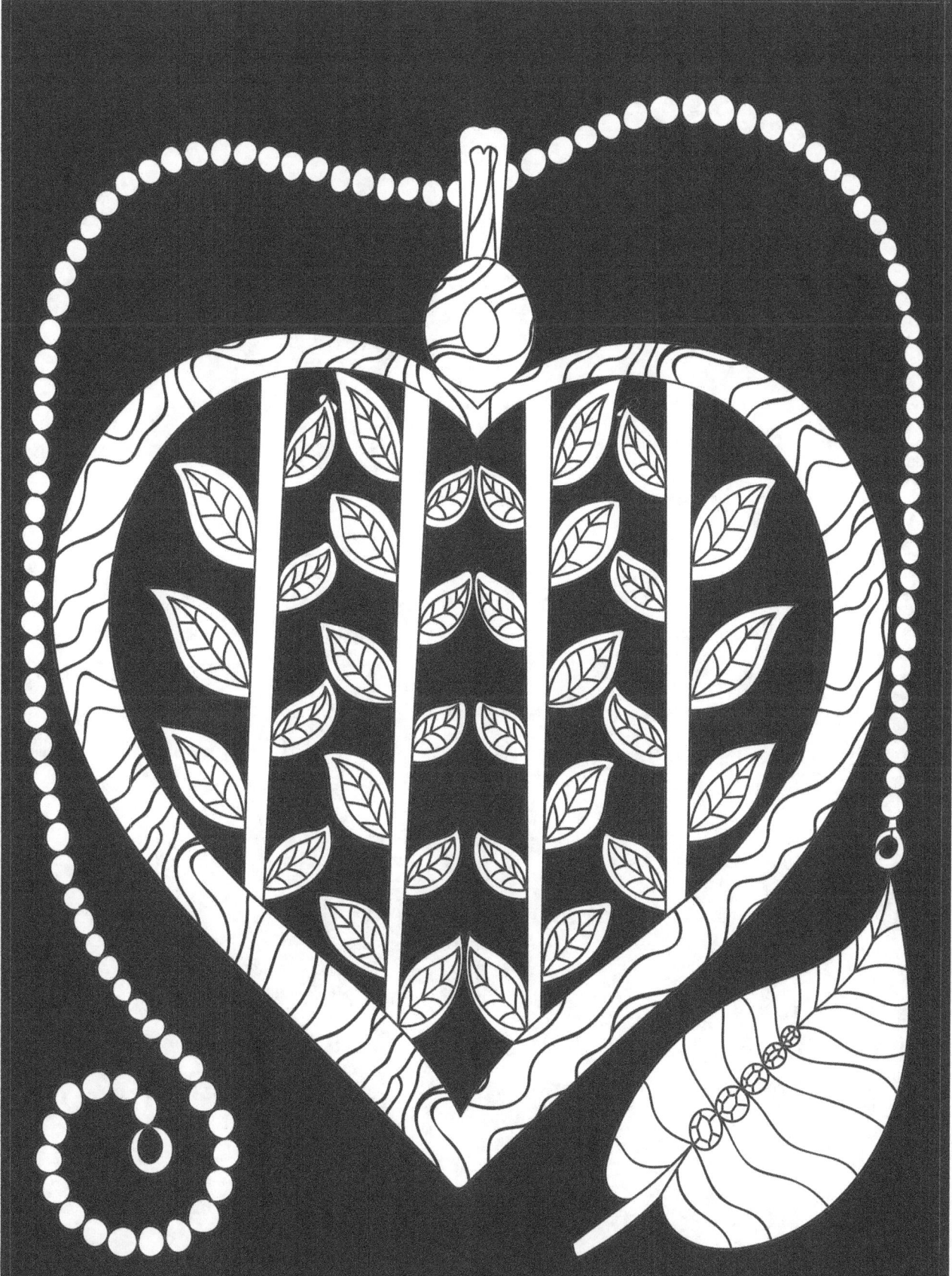

PRETTY LITTLE THINGS

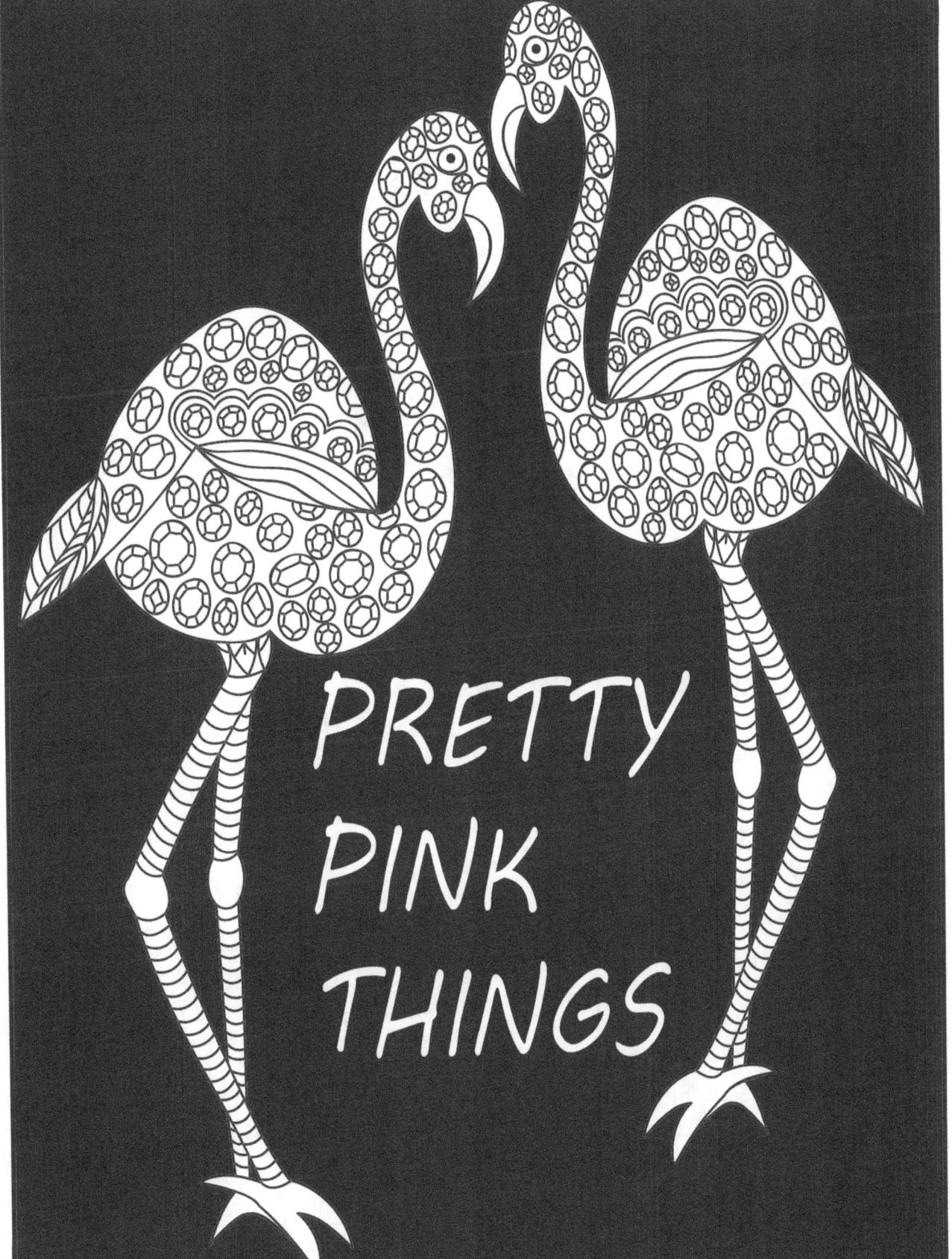

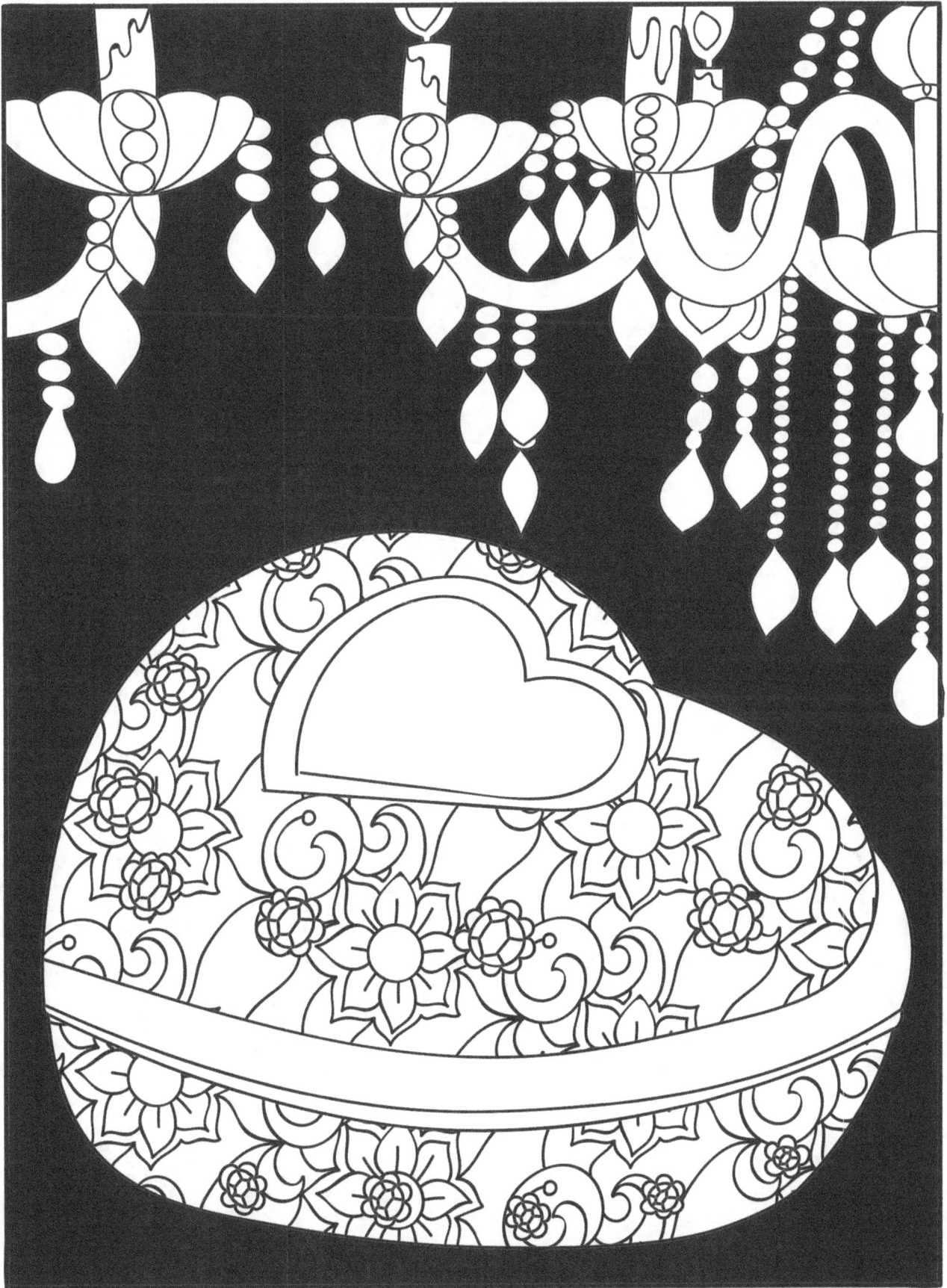

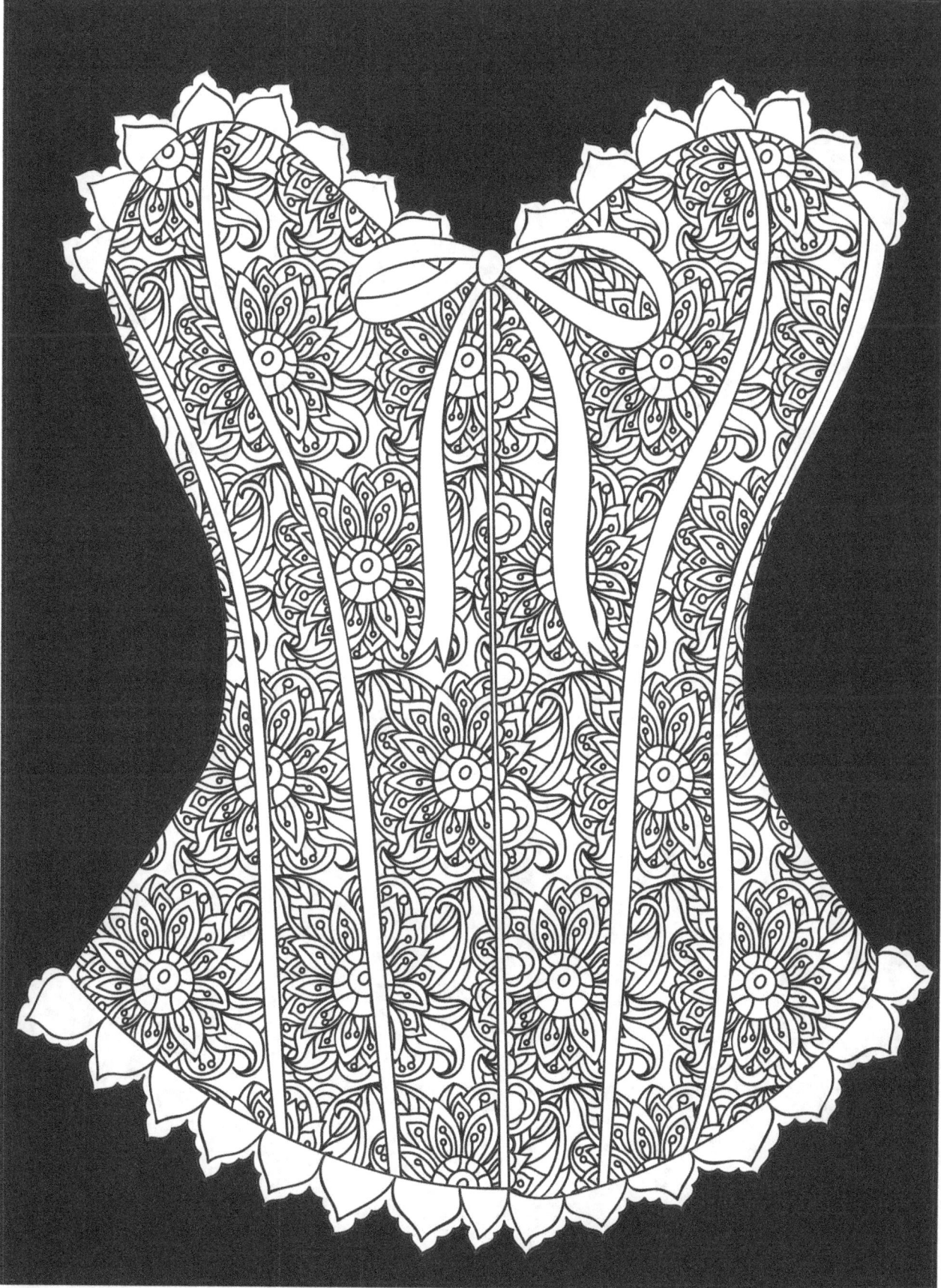

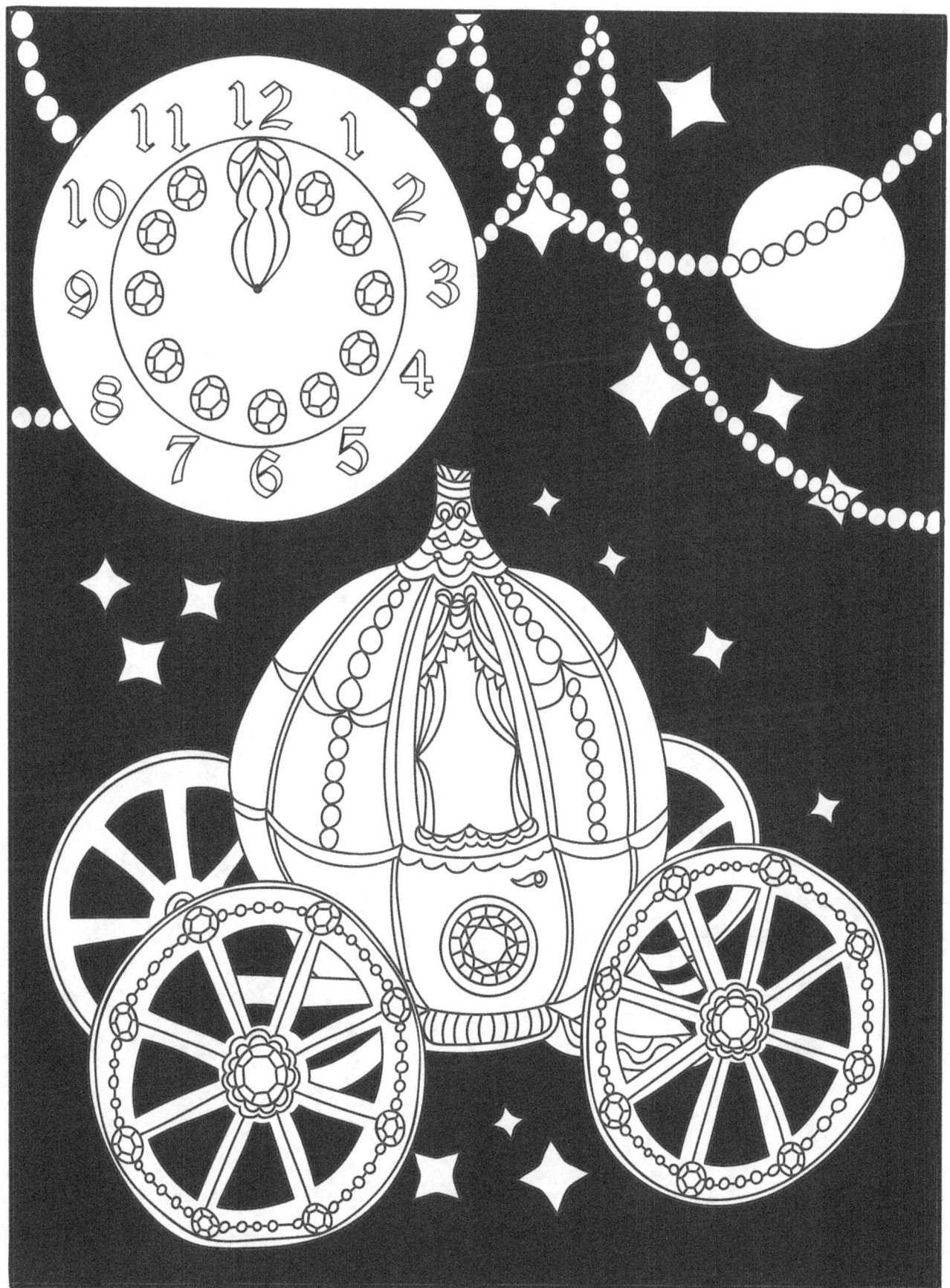

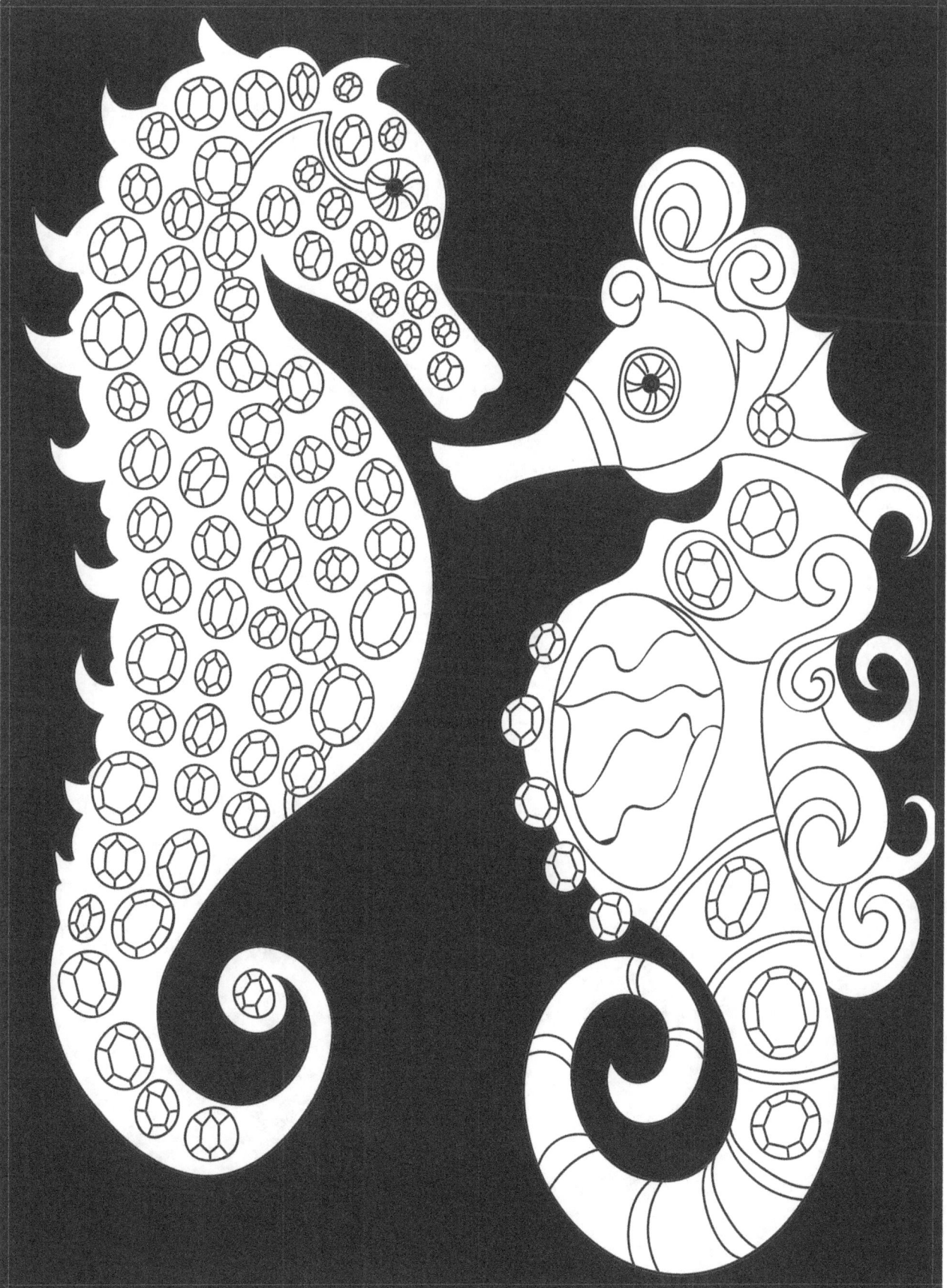

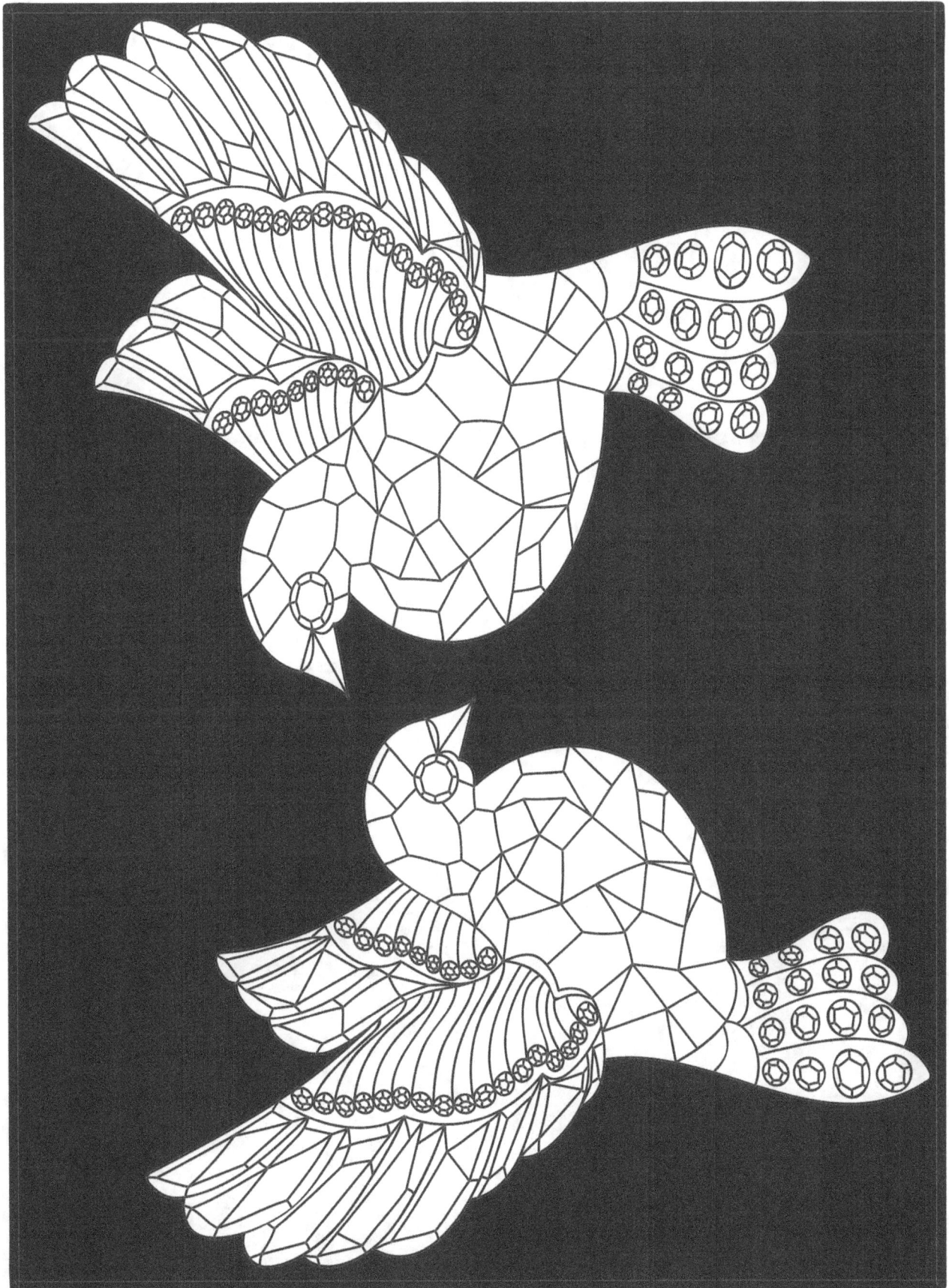

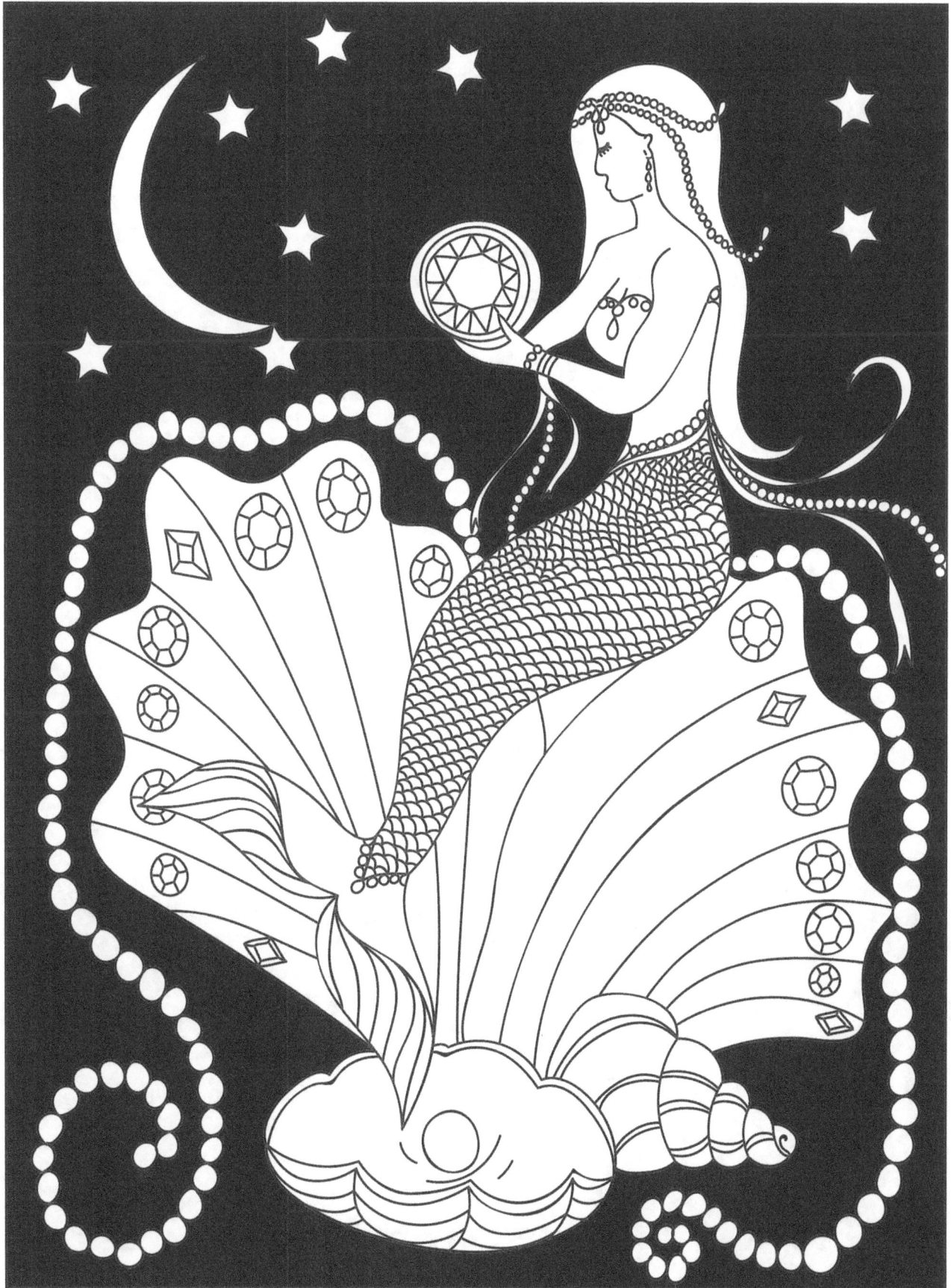

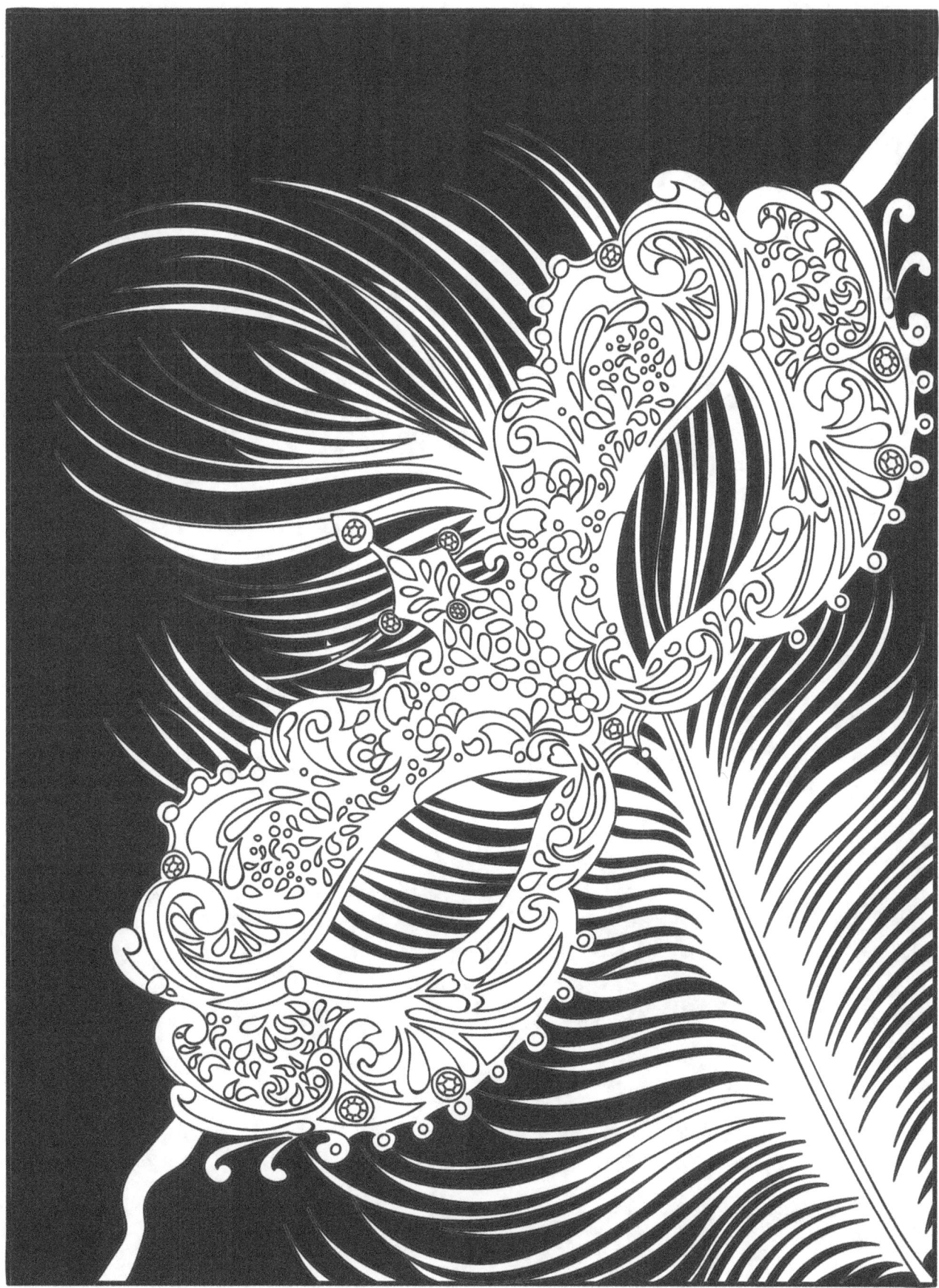

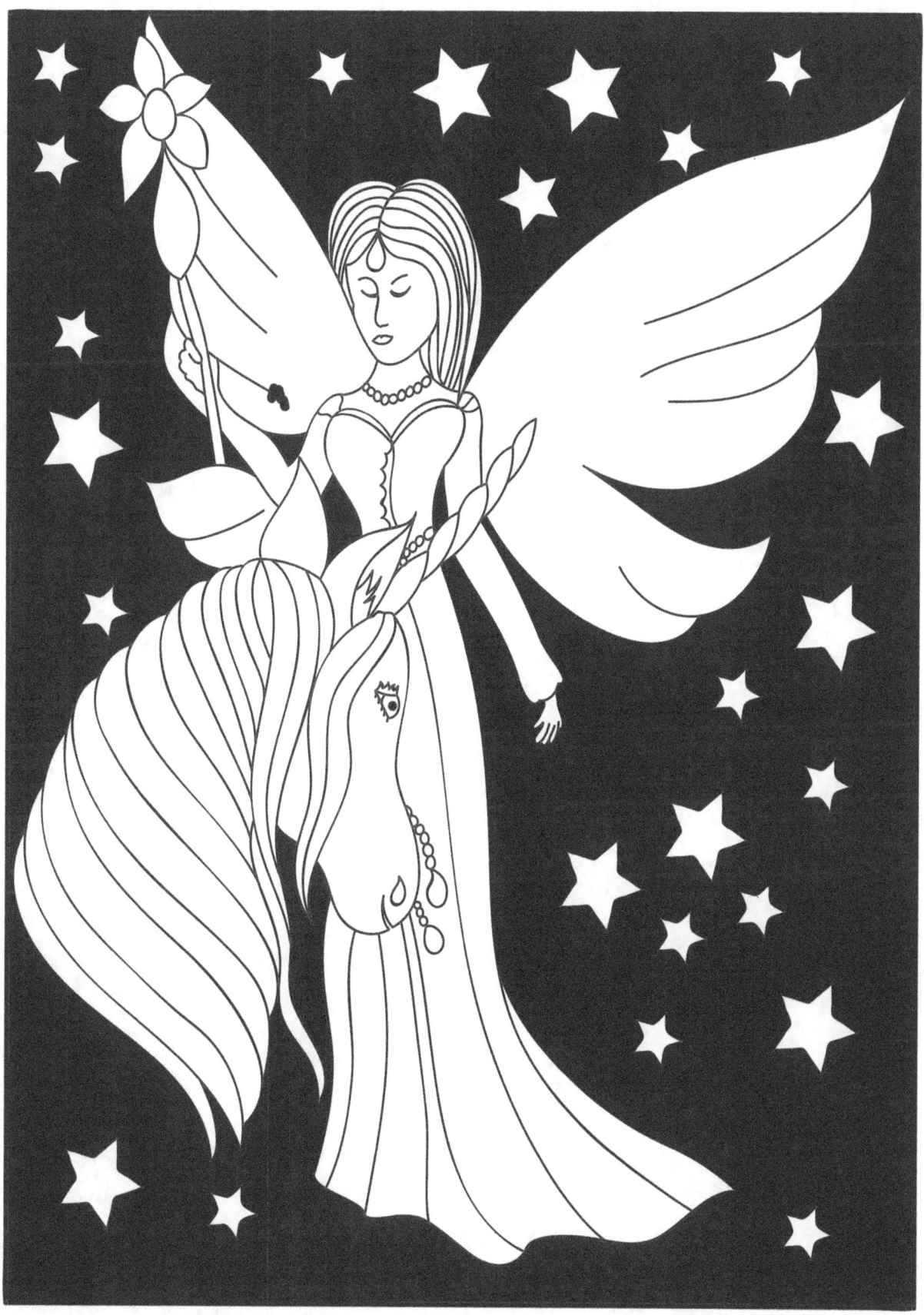

COLOR TEST PAGE

COLOR TEST PAGE

www.ingramcontent.com/pod-product-compliance
Lightning Source LLC
Chambersburg PA
CBHW081016170526
45158CB00010B/3057